THE UNITED STATES IN BIBLE PROPHECY? A SURMISE!

STEFAN DAVID STARR

ISBN 979-8-88832-327-4 (paperback)
ISBN 979-8-88832-328-1 (digital)

Christian Faith Publishing
832 Park Avenue
Meadville, PA 16335
www.christianfaithpublishing.com

Printed in the United States of America

This book is about the threat to Israel and to America, mainly from Communist China, Russia, Iran, Ethiopia, and Libya. Bible prophecy or eschatology in the New Testament is much more implied, compared to the Old Testament in the book of Ezekiel 38–39. This is because the Roman government censors would have shredded the book of Revelation/Apocalypse (a series of letters from the Isle of Patmos, in the Mediterranean Ocean). Ezekiel 38–39 is much more detailed in who and what will happen to the enemies of Israel from the north (Russia) and from the east (Iran), also from Africa (Ethiopia, Libya, and Algeria?). In the beginning of the Holy Bible, including the New Testament, there were no chapters and verses divided up. The Bible first contained only oral (spoken) traditional stories.

First John 5:14 says, "Now this is the confidence that we have in [God], that if we ask anything according to His will, He hears us." My opinion does not really matter; it is only God's opinion that matters ultimately. First Corinthians 8:01 says, "Knowledge Puffeth up, but love builds up!" In the winter of 2022, it is theoretically possible for Communist Chinese troops to march across the Alaskan ice to first invade Alaskan airspace, then into Canada, and then to our forty-eight states! This is my conviction; it has been reported by several news agencies that the Chinese are and have built artificial islands in the Pacific Ocean to land military aircraft upon (TBN's [Trinity Broadcasting Network] *Centerpoint* & other media outlets)! The Russian Federation lost many of its affiliated republics and army troops (the Warsaw Pact) after the Europeans saw the fall of the Soviet Union. This helps the US Monroe Doctrine!

The Monroe Doctrine is in the eighth edition of *Black's Law Dictionary*. It reads:

> The principle that the United States will allow no intervention or domination by any Non-American nation in the Western hemisphere. This principle, which has some recognition in international law [though not as a formal doctrine], was first announced by President James Monroe in 1823 "The Monroe Doctrine is a policy which the United States has followed in her own interest more or less consistently for more than a century, and in itself is not contrary to international law, though possible applications of it might easily be so. But it certainly is not a rule of international law. It is comparable to policies such as the "balance of power" in Europe, or the British policies of maintaining the Independence of Belgium or the security of our sea-routes to the East, or the former Japanese claim to something like a paramount influence over developments in the Far East Ap Apart from other objections, it is impossible to regard as a rule of law a doctrine which the United States claims the sole right to interpret, which she applies only as and when she chooses. Nor is the doctrine, as Article Twenty-one of the Covenant described it, a "regional understanding, for the other states of the region

concerned, that is to say, the Continent of America, have never been parties to it and indeed have often resented it." (J. L. Brierly, *The Law of Nations*, page 314, fifth edition, 1955)

Our allies will be the United Nations, the North Atlantic Treaty Organization (OTAN in the French language), the Organization of American States (a *mini*-mini-American UN-like government body covering Alaska to Argentina), and also, the African Union (which I assume is for the Free World). The term *Second World* refers exclusively to the Marxist-Leninist-Maoist-Communist world. The term the *Third World* refers to nation-states that are impoverished and are not under Communist control. A massive counterinvasion by a UN member, such as New Delhi (India), would need one billion rifles to counter the one billion rifles of Communist China! There is power in numbers basically. These rifles would not be stationed all in one geographic location globally. So I am writing about—you guessed it—World War III!

Thanks to human nature, this will definitely happen in our lifetimes! Our last interplanetary exploration will probably be a joint mission to Mars. All the other planets are probably composed only of gases and have no solid core and have extreme bad visibility, such as Venus. Mars has great visibility and a clear visibility.

Mars and Mercury have hard surfaces, but Mercury is right next to the extremely hot star or sun in the Milky Way, (our) solar system (*Random House Dictionary*, a large edition). The rest of our planets are only gasses, from what I have heard. The names for outer space explorers are astronauts (USA), cosmonauts (Russia), and taikonauts (China). Since it takes a whole year to go to Mars only, the Earth will not be able to send humans past it! Under President Donald Trump, the sixth branch of the US military was founded. The US Space Force came from the US Air Force. To me, it is redundant, because the US Air Force was already being used to test X-planes or purely experimental aircraft. One of the USAF bases that tested experimental military jets was where the US space shuttles landed from outer space for the most part. The place which I am writing about is Edwards Air Force Base in California's Mohave Desert in southeastern California. Some of the space shuttle missions were military in nature.

Now, back to Earth, Terra Firma, and our oceans and seas. Revelation 9:14–16 mentions the Euphrates River. Revelation 9:16 mentions a two-hundred-million-man army! Revelation 16:12, 16–21 implies that there will be a long "long march" (Mao Tse-Tung coined this expression) from Beijing/Peking to the Mediterranean Ocean. Only there is just one problem. It is called the Free World! The Euphrates River, which ends at Baghdad, Iraq, becomes the Shatt al-Arab River with the Tigris River (just east of the Euphrates River!)

The Shatt al-Arab River flows into the Persian Gulf, near Iran. This is where the Babylonian Empire was located. At the end of Revelation chapter 16 and 17, there is a definite reference to Babylon. In Revelation 17:5, there is a woman with an inscription on her forehead that goes like this, "Mystery, Babylon the great, the mother of prostitutes and of the abominations of the earth."

Right now, as it stands, the Free World would have a nuclear war over an invasion of Iraq by China and Asia. The USA and the rest of the Free World is definitely blocking the Axis Powers in the east, such as Russia as well as China and Iran! The Euphrates River mysteriously disappears in Revelation 16:12, and then Asia marches to attempt to conquer the God and real estate of Israel! The Euphrates River *flows from* Turkey and ends at Baghdad, Iraq. Right now, the top "global cop" is the USA, standing guard along with most of the UN. The UN is not a pure organization though. Russia and China have permanent veto power in the UN's Security Council (refer to the UN Charter in the eighth edition of *Black's Law Dictionary*). During the Harry S. Truman administration, the United Nations was started in San Francisco, California, in 1945 (*Black's Law Dictionary*, eighth edition). In May of 1947, the State of Israel was resurrected and founded. Both the UN and Israel have two things in common: they both stand for the rule of law and have blue-and-white-colored flags only! The UN and the Republic of Israel are made of clay. Israel is not currently a theocratic state run by God. Their legislature is called the Knesset. Tel Aviv is where they used to meet. President Trump was able to have Jerusalem be reestablished as Israel's capital once again. My point is that human law is like wet clay and the Holy Bible has eternally fixed laws that never change.

> Jesus Christ is the same yesterday, today and
> forever. (Hebrews 13:8)

The King James Version in the epistle of James 1:8 says, "A double-minded man is unstable in all his ways." James 4:8 says, "Draw High (near) to God, and He will draw nigh to you. Cleanse your hands, ye sinners; and purify your hearts, ye doubleminded." Our political leaders are very two-faced; this is why I believe our governmental system is in such bad shape! Our priorities are not specific enough for sound decisions. Without the US Supreme Court (governed by laws and not agendas), we would only have either anarchy or a political zoo! Federalism is the best human governmental system: it got the USA to the moon and back safely! The US Declaration of Independence was inspired by the Holy Trinity in my opinion! The First Amendment to the US Constitution is found in Revelation 22:11–12 KJV (1611):

> He that is unjust, let him be unjust still: and
> he which is filthy, let him be filthy still: and he
> that is righteous, let him be righteous still: and he
> that is holy, let him be holy still. And, behold, I
> come quickly; and my reward is with me, to give
> every man according as his works shall be.

The US First Amendment neither rules God in or out: but God and his people are not endorsed or condemned by the US government. Church politics is not endorsed by the US government. The church of Jesus Christ is only the Bride of Christ, not the groom! Second Corinthians 5:21 says, "He who knew no sin, became sin, that we might be made the righteousness of God in Him." The Holy Trinity is never to be blamed! Only mere *Homo sapiens* / human beings are! We as Christians are always considered to be a "work in progress" (anonymous). We as the church must strive to grow as believers. In First Corinthians 13:13, it says, "So Faith, Hope and Love Abide, these three; but the greatest of these is Love." Please notice that faith and hope are political; but is love political? This is definitely a gray area! In the English language, there is only one word for love. But in the original New Testament Koine Greek, there are several! The Greek word for divine love is *agape*. *Philia* is brotherly love, *storge* is parental love, and *eros* is sexual love. The devil cannot imitate love or better show love; all he and his minions can do is unsuccessfully mimic God and his people! First John 4:19 says, "We love Him, because He first loved us." This is the church and the world being touched by the Holy Trinity / Jesus / God.

Love can be shrewd. Second Samuel 22:27–31 NIV reads:

> To the pure you show yourself pure, but to the crooked you show yourself shrewd. You save the humble, but your eyes are on the haughty to bring them low. You are my Lamp, O Lord; the Lord turns my darkness into light. As for God, His way is perfect; the word of th the Lord is flawless. He is a shield for all who take refuge in Him.

Ephesians 3:17 says that we must be "rooted and grounded in love." Ephesians 4:15 is the diplomatic verse; it reads, "But, speaking the truth in love, that we might grow up into Him (Jesus) who is the head of the Church." Ephesians 5:21 reads, "Submitting to one another out of the reverence for Christ." This is the teamwork verse in the Holy Bible! Governmentally speaking, the term is called comity (not comedy; that is a mnemonic in order to help you remember the word *comity*). In *Black's Law Dictionary*, comity is as follows:

1. A practice among political entities (as nations, states, or courts of different jurisdictions), involving especially mutual recognition of legislative, executive, and judicial acts—also termed Comitas Gentium (Courtoisie Internationale [the French Language] page 284, *Black's Law Dictionary*, Eighth Edition). Comity, "in the legal sense, is neither a matter of absolute obligation, on the one hand, nor of mere courtesy and good will, upon the other. But it is the recognition which one nation allows within its territory to the legislative, executive or Judicial acts of another nation, having due regard both to international duty and convenience, and to the rights of its own citizens, or of other persons who are under the protection of its laws." (Hilton V. Guyot, Volume 159 U.S. 113, 163–164 [point pages], 16 S. CT. 139, 143 [1895])

2. International Law. This sense is considered a misusage: "[In] Anglo-American jurisprudence…the term is also misleadingly found to be used as a synonym for international law." (Peter Macalister-Smith, "comity," in the *Encyclopedia of Public International*

> *Law*, Page 672 [1992]) Comity Clause: the
> clause of the US Constitution giving citizens
> of one states the right to all privileges and
> immunities enjoyed by citizens of the other
> states (US Constitution, Article IV, Section
> Two, Clause One.," page 284 of *Black's Law
> Dictionary*, Eighth Edition).

Another example of this is that the USA and the Dominion of Canada share English as a common language and also have the Old King James Version of the Bible as another cultural similarity (the KJV Bible, the United Kingdom of AD 1611). Someone once said that "many hands make the load light!" That is why we will always need foreign allies. US President Trump's "America first" / go-it-alone philosophy is very naive and impractical. It is like not exchanging favors with a close friend or a good neighbor. Unfortunately, we will always have bad domestic and international nation-state neighbors. Also, watch out for the United States of Europe as predicted by the apostle John. It involves 666, evil government, consolidation of international power, and the Mark of the Beast, which means an individual or group cannot buy or sell without the permission of the government. US federalism currently protects the US citizen from such a blatantly evil global power grab! Luke 11:18 says basically that if "Satan's kingdom is divided, it will have an end." Armageddon is probably an East/West struggle for power in which Jesus needs to step in and stop the human race from killing itself (Billy Graham sermon).

Back to today's situation. China, Russia, and Iran—today's bad guys for Israel, America, and the free world—are definitely strengthening their alliances. I have seen this my own eyes in television news reports.

If the bad guys can learn the fellow bad guys' foreign language, the least we could do is learn at least a little foreign language skills from our neighbors in the NATO, UN, and other countries. I personally have studied a little German and Russian in college—also, informally French and a little Spanish. I am by no means perfect, but it helps to identify where people came from and maybe what they are talking about next to me! The Earth is like a neighborhood. There are your friends and neighbors and "sandpaper-people" (anonymous), whom you just cannot stand to be around.

It was reported by the *Wall Street Journal* on May 6, 2019, that President Trump was for tariffs on Chinese goods; in my opinion, the only reason President Trump was elected is because he was the only candidate who spoke up against China. The Bush dynasty and the Clinton dynasty treated China as though the Chinese Communists are our equal! Talk about megalomania—the Chinese, the Russians, and the Iranians are the new Nazi Party. They may have a different ideology, but they are supporting the devil and his minions! Trump made a serious blunder when he ignored the *de minimis policy* that was in place, and still might be. It exempts people/individuals from paying the tariff by having their merchandise go directly from China to a specific domestic US address! This a hole in the life raft of US government law enforcement and creates wasting time for everyone! Legitimate governmental precedents do not create a waste of time; God never wastes his time. Of course, we will never be able to do what God can do all the time; we are only finite and mortal, but we ought to use each precious moment in our lives with a good purpose and not squander God's time and ours!

The God of the Bible is not a republic and will never be a democratic-republican "structure" if you will. If we follow what the Bible says, "pray without ceasing and give thanks in all circumstances, for this is God's will for you in Christ, Jesus" (1 Thessalonians 5:17–18 NIV).

As time goes on for every Christian, the greater is the pull to force people to obey the government and not God. It probably comes and goes in cycles, as it always has been. In God's courtroom, there are no backroom or shady operations, such as the money changers at the national temple of Israel, where Jesus drove out the commercial side of the Jewish faith and started the fulfilment of Old Testament prophecy (Matthew 12:12 and Mark 11:15)! Jesus Christ's kingdom is not a rat race like this world. Matthew 7:24–27 speaks of building upon a rock—the Rock that is Jesus! *Stare decisis* is like it; it means letting the prior precedent stand. I suppose that is the goal in secular law. Things which are closest to Jesus are probably the best course of action. Such as what Ecclesiastes 9:4 says, "He who is joined to all the living has hope, but better a live dog than a dead lion." We as mere mortals tend to be "dead lions" much of the time! Psalm 24:1 in the KJV says, "The Earth is the Lord's and the fulness thereof." Psalm 2:1–8 reads:

> Why do the nations conspire [against the God and Nation of Israel] and the peoples plot in vain? The kings of the Earth take their stand the rulers gather together against the Lord and against His Anointed One. "Let us break their chains," they say, "and throw off their fetters." The One enthroned in Heaven laughs; the Lord scoffs at them. Then He [God] rebukes them in his anger and terrifies them in His wrath, saying, "I have installed My King on Zion (Jesus of Nazareth, Apocalypse 16:17–18), My Holy Hill." I will proclaim the decree of the Lord: He said to me, "You are My Son; today I have become your Father. Ask of Me, and I will make the nations for your inheritance, the ends of the Earth your and the Lord's possession." (Psalm 2:1–8 NIV)

Romans 8:17 states that we are "joint heirs" with Christ Jesus. Back to Psalm 2:9–12:

> You will rule them with an iron scepter [*Webster's New Collegiate Dictionary* says that a *scepter* is a "baton or staff borne or carried by a sovereign as an emblem of authority"; also, royal or imperial authority; sovereignty; to endow with the scepter; invest with royal authority.], you will dash them to pieces like pottery. Therefore, you kings, be wise; be warned, you rulers of the Earth. Serve the Lord with fear and rejoice with trembling. Kiss the Son Jesus Christ, lest ["so that"] He won't be angry and you won't be destroyed in your way, for His wrath can flare up in a moment. Blessed are all who take refuge in Him [Jesus, the Anointed Messiah of Israel and the rest of the world].

Jesus Christ's Great White Throne judgment is final and unending. So please avoid it by making Jesus your Boss/The Holy Trinity. He will then give you his peace. Numbers 6:22–27 is the Aaronic Blessing.

> May the Lord bless you and keep you. May the Lord smile on you and be gracious to you. May the Lord show you His favor and give you [His] Peace ["*Shalom*" in Hebrew].
> Whenever Aaron and his sons bless the People of Israel in my name, I The Lord God of Israel] will Bless them. (Numbers 6:24–27 NLT)

Now Ezekiel 38:1–6 reads:

> The word of the Lord came to me: Son of
> Man, set your face against Gog, of the Land of
> Magog, the Chief Prince of Meshech and Tubal;
> prophecy against him and say: This is what the
> Sovereign Lord says: I am against you, O Gog,
> Chief Prince of Meshech and Tubal. I will turn
> you around, put hooks in your jaws and bring
> you out with your whole army—Your horses,
> your horsemen fully armed, and a great horde
> with large a and small shields, all of them bran-
> dishing [*Webster's Dictionary*, "to shake or wave"]
> their swords. Persia [Iran], Ethiopia and Lybia
> with them [possibly part of Algeria also]. Also,
> Gomer with all its troops, and Beth Togarmah
> from the Far North [Slavic peoples, viz., Russia]
> with all its troops—the many nations with you.

In Ezekiel 38:18, God will do a Psalm 2 on them. He will kill
them by his supernatural wrath! Since Jesus and the rest of the Triune
God is invisible, supernatural, and a spiritual power, he (the Holy
Trinity) cannot be killed by a physical weapon or any weapon devised
by mankind! Jesus was born because of a supernatural decision, not an
act of human sexual will. Jesus Christ's death on the cross of Calvary
was only temporary. That means he can go anywhere in the universe /
our solar system, anywhere without dying permanently. According to
the Judeo-Christian faith, the man called Jesus can defeat any political, economic, religious, or evil plot against him! According to Isaiah
40:8, "the grass withereth, the flowers fadeth/fall, but the Word of
our God shall stand forever!" Psalm 119:89 KJV reads, "Your Word,
O Lord stands forever, it is forever settled in Heaven." Psalm 119:100
NIV states, "I have more understanding than [the human] elders,

for I obey your precepts [principles]." Matthew 7:13–14 KJV states, "Wide is the gate, and broad is the way that leadeth to destruction. But narrow is the road that leadeth to life, and few that be who find it." It is also being specific about one's goals in life that helps avoid the broad and direction-specific focus that we as Christians need. If we are all over the map, like a chicken with its head cut off, this situation is never really any good for people. When I went to college to obtain my bachelor of arts degree in political science in May of 1989, I kept myself from being overcommitted with extracurricular activities! Campus Crusade for Christ (now called CRU), the Baptist Student Union, and political activity were all I ever focused upon. I never went to any sporting events.

Personally, I would rather participate in sports than watch them; also, I never had a television in my apartment when I was going to California State University, Chico, from August 1987 through May 21, 1989. Also, I graduated as fast as possible, because my grade point average was dropping like a rock. So I only have a major in political science, with no minor subject of study. Since my degree is from a state college, the degree is forever on file, unless, of course there is a manipulation by an Antichrist who wants to alter reality in order to create a false narrative, and that is what the communists or fascists or anti-Semites do under their rule and reign! I am a Jewish German American, so I personally know a little bit about people who are legends in their own mind, such as Austrian Adolph Hitler and Mao Tse-Tung, *arbeit macht frei*, or the half-truth "Work makes freedom." Our nation has it very good right now, so elect leaders who have integrity and principles. There are always too few unfortunately! As a result of human/human nature, Bible prophecy/eschatology will come to pass! In Ezekiel 39:9–10, it says that there will be so many weapons that have wooden parts that it will not be necessary to burn any tree branches for seven years! "They will plunder those who plundered them and loot those who looted them, declares the sovereign Lord" (Ezekiel 39: 9–10

NIV). Where Gog and his supporters will be buried will be called the Valley of Hamon Gog (Ezekiel 39:11 NIV). Ezekiel 39:12 states that it will take seven months to completely bury the troops that tried to invade and kill the nation of Israel. It also says in the same passage of the Holy Scripture that some people's remains will be missed, such as a bone or two; then the burying of human remains will be completed after seven months. Revelation 20:6 states that Jesus Christ will reign for approximately 365,000 sunrises, plus leap years. For the one-thousand-year reign of Jesus Christ. Compared to the rest of human history, that is not much time to live in a heaven-reigning-world! Most of human history is unfortunately a very sad story because of what humans have done to each other! In the Beatitudes in Matthew 5 and Luke 6, Thomas has doubts about Jesus being raised from the dead. The very nature of human government is not conducive to being able to do great things, unless much thought is involved, such as the Great Wall of China, the Egyptian Pyramids, Hanging Gardens of Babylon, etc. Jesus Christ is and will be supernatural from his very beginning to *his* never-ending "end"!

What starts out as only mortal thoughts tends to be merely human ideas. The ability for God to perform miracles for the Jews and the church globally is never mere human experience. Whether it is the parting of the Red Sea in the Middle East, Lourdes in the kingdom of France and affecting the French people, from the most lowly Ms. Bernadette Soubirous to royalty in France who needed a miracle from Jesus and God of the Bible, to the rigorous process of canonizing people in the Roman Catholic Church, God's promises are all yea and Amen" in [God]. AMEN.

(Second Corinthians 1:20). The word *promise* appears thirteen times in the King James Concordance of the Old King James Bible (*Strong's Exhaustive Concordance of the Bible*, James Strong, LLD (a jurisprudence degree), and a Systematic Theological Doctorate of the Bible, Fully Revised and Corrected by John R. Kohlenberger III and James Swanson, Zondervan, Grand Rapids, Michigan 49530, USA).

Our nation alone in fighting China, Russia, and Iran would require either a miracle to survive an attack or foreign allied military assistance. These forces have moral sin imbedded in them, because of the fall of Adam and Eve, otherwise known as human nature! That is probably why I do not trust centralized government systems, unless these are directly governed either by the Holy Bible or eternally proven-to-be-true-documents, such as the US Declaration of Independence! Because of our alliance with Napoleon Bonaparte and because of Divine Providence, we became a superpower in the early twentieth century!

Explorers have not all been Christians, but the USA has been blessed to have many: George Washington Carver, who discovered the many uses of the peanut; the Wright Brothers, who invented the first biplane airplane; and of course, Thomas Alva Edison, the inventor of the light bulb, phonograph, and the idea of the motion picture. He said that the light bulb "was 99 percent perspiration and 1 percent inspiration!" Our enemy, the Soviet Union, was able to beat us into outer space with the ball and antenna known as Sputnik, which means "fellow traveler" (a slang name for a Communist), "companion"; Planet, secondary planet (*Russian-English Dictionary* compiled by Professor V. K. Mueller, 60,000 words, third edition, revised and enlarged by E. P. Dutton & Company Incorporated, tenth printing, April, 1958, page 666. Just like the old Greek Aesop fable about the tortoise and the hare (rabbit), we beat the Soviet Union to the moon's surface. Through the many companies which aided technical advances which helped the USA's quest to the lunar surface, we as a society have a greater standard of living due to taking risks as illustrated in the parable of the talents in the Bible in which the three stewards were encouraged to invest and gain more economic returns (Matthew 25:14–30). Basically, there were three stewards in this parable from Jesus. One received five talents, invested, and received five more. The second steward received two talents and, after investing, received two more talents or monetary units. Their master was very pleased, but the third steward never took any investment risks and hid his master's money to be invested in the earth; he buried it (Matthew 25:25). This angered the master, and he told his people to give the one hidden talent to the one with ten talents (Matthew 25:28–30). Jesus said that the master in the parable, called the non-risk-taker, is a "worthless servant." He said (rather harshly) to throw that worthless steward or servant outside, into the darkness, where there will be weeping and gnashing of teeth (Matthew 25:30).

Only a few teachers of wisdom, such as Aesop, Socrates, Plato, and Aristotle, have come close, but not surpassed, the wisdom found in the Holy Bible. Chances are, the Greek fables are found in some form in Bible stories or are a great addition to the Bible, although the book of Revelation 22:18–19 says not to add or take away from the Holy Bible. In other words, the Bible is complete by itself; in order for God to be God, he definitely must be entirely complete. About China and Asia, if it quacks like a duck and gives biblical clues, then I have to suspect that the God of the Holy Bible is involved with this world's human history to some extent. I do not have a fixed percentage though! "The grace of God is amazing to me!"

> *For the Law [Torah] was given through Moses; but*
> *grace and truth were given through Jesus Christ.*
>
> —John 1:17

ABOUT THE AUTHOR

S tefan David Starr grew up and lives in Carmel Valley, California. He has a BA in political science degree from Chico State (1989). He has been a born-again Christian since August 1, 1984.

www.ingramcontent.com/pod-product-compliance
Lightning Source LLC
Chambersburg PA
CBHW022047150726
47990CB00004B/1641